LIVING WATER

THE POWER OF
THE HOLY SPIRIT
IN YOUR LIFE

STUDY GUIDE

All Study material has been written by:
Jim and June Hesterly

Acts 1:8 Ministries, Inc.
P.O. Box 28771
Santa Ana, CA 92704

Copyright © 2000 by James L. Hesterly

Published by Acts 1:8 Ministries, Inc.
P.O. Box 28771
Santa Ana, CA 92704

Library of Congress Cataloging in Publication Data
Hesterly, James L.

ISBN 1-928779-01-8

Taken From: Living Water By Chuck Smith
Copyright © 1996 by Harvest House Publishers,
Eugene, Oregon
Used by permission

This Workbook has been designed to be used in conjunction with the book *Living Water*, written by Pastor Chuck Smith. It can be used in small groups, classroom situations or personal studies. Each question can be answered by referring to the text *Living Water* and by reading all scriptural references given.

All study material has been written by:

Jim and June Hesterly

Acts 1:8 Ministries, Inc.

P.O. Box 28771

Santa Ana, CA 92704

(714) 641-7132

TABLE OF CONTENTS

LESSON ONE

As you begin your study:

Always start with prayer, looking to the Holy Spirit for His guidance as you observe, interpret, and apply each lesson to your life.

1. Carefully read through Chapter 1, "Personality Plus", page 11.

2. Explain the word "comfortless" in John 14:18.

_____

_____

_____

3. What was the promise given to us in John 14:16-18?

_____

_____

_____

4. Who is the Holy Spirit? _____

_____

_____

5. List the characteristics of the Holy Spirit given in:

   a. 1 Corinthians 2:10,11 _____

   b. 1 Corinthians 12:11 _____

   c. Ephesians 4:30 _____

   d. Romans 15:30 _____

   e. John 15:26 _____

   f. John 16:13_____

6. Many personal treatments are accorded to the Holy Spirit. What

examples do we have in:

a. Acts 5 _____

_____

b. Acts 7:51 _____

_____

c. Mark 3:28 _____

_____

7. How does the Holy Spirit act as a Person?

a. _____

b. _____

c. _____

d. _____

e. _____

f. _____

8. Why are these facts important to us? _____

_____

_____

9. Describe a personal experience of the Holy Spirit's guidance in your
life. _____

_____

_____

10. As we seek the Holy Spirit, our goal should never be _____

_____

but to _____

LESSON TWO

1. Carefully read through Chapter 2, "The Mystery of the Three in One", page 23.

2. According to the scriptures, how is God manifested in the Trinity?

a. _____

b. _____

c. _____

3. If we deny the Trinity what else must we deny?_____

_____

4. How many times is the Holy Spirit mentioned in the Old Testament and what names are used? _____

_____

_____

5. Compare Genesis 1:1 with Genesis 1:26. What Hebrew word is used for God and what is the form used?_____

_____

_____

6. Read Isaiah 6:3. Why is the word "Holy" used three times and what is its significance? _____

_____

_____

7. What can we say with confidence concerning the Holy Spirit?

_____

_____

_____

8. List the attributes of the Holy Spirit given in:

a. Hebrews 9:14 _____

b. Psalms 139:7-10 _____

c. 1 Corinthians 2:10,11 _____

d. Luke 1:35 _____

9. What are the works of Deity? _____

_____

_____

10. How does God speak? _____

_____

_____

_____

11. Explain how the Holy Spirit helps us. _____

_____

_____

_____

12. How has the Holy Spirit spoken to you? _____

_____

_____

_____

LESSON THREE

1. Carefully read through Chapter 3, "At Work in the World," page 35.

2. According to John 16:7-11, what are the three tasks of the Holy Spirit in the world? _____

_____

_____

3. Why did Jesus say that the Holy Spirit will reprove the world of sin?

_____

_____

_____

4. How is the Holy Spirit blasphemed and how can we avoid committing this sin? _____

_____

_____

5. What is your personal relationship with Jesus Christ and how did you arrive at this conclusion? _____

_____

_____

6. Give a brief explanation of sin and righteousness.

_____

_____

_____

7. Explain God's standard for righteousness and how we are able to meet that standard. _____

_____

8. Why is it important to us that Jesus defeated the principalities and powers of darkness as explained in Colossians 2:13-15?

_____

_____

_____

9. In what ways should this have an effect on our lives?

a. _____

_____

b. _____

_____

c. _____

_____

d. _____

_____

e. _____

_____

f. _____

_____

LESSON FOUR

1. Carefully read through Chapter 4, "Keeping the Lid On", page 47.

2. According to 2 Thessalonians 2:3-7, there is One who is restraining evil in our world. Who is this One and what is His task? _____

_____

_____

3. Describe the conflict that Christians face in the world and how we have been weakened in the battle. _____

_____

_____

4. Why are Christians called to be "salt"? _____

_____

_____

5. Briefly describe the strategy of Satan and his purpose.

_____

_____

_____

6. Who is hindering the work of the enemy and how is this being accomplished?_____

_____

_____

7. Describe the type of battle we are in and the weapons we have been given to succeed._____

_____

_____

8. How can we be a purifying influence in the world and be a faithful testimony? _____

_____

_____

9. Briefly write down your own personal testimony.

_____

_____

_____

_____

10. Because Jesus Christ will one day establish His Kingdom, we can expect it to be filled with:

a. _____

_____

b. _____

_____

c. _____

_____

d. _____

_____

"Even so, come quickly, Lord Jesus."

LESSON FIVE

1. Carefully read through Chapter 5, "The Church's Divine Helper", page 59.

2. What causes a church to succeed and function correctly?

_____

_____

_____

3. Briefly describe the vision given to Peter that is recorded in Acts 11:1-10.

_____

_____

_____

4. What were the results of Peter's obedience to the Holy Spirit's leading?

_____

_____

_____

5. How was the ministry of Paul and Barnabas effected by the direction of the Holy Spirit? _____

_____

_____

6. In what ways are we led by the Holy Spirit today?

_____

_____

_____

_____

7. Compare the generosity of the early church to the story of Ananias and his wife, Sapphira.

Early Church—Acts 4:32-37	Ananais & Sapphira—Acts 5:1-11

8. What purpose did the Holy Spirit have in protecting the early church from the sin of hypocrisy? _____

_____

_____

9. Explain one of the key works of the Holy Spirit in the church and His purpose. _____

_____

_____

10. Why was the early church successful? _____

_____

_____

11. What is the "tragic mistake of the modern church"?

_____

_____

_____

12. How can we be all that God wants His church to be?

_____

_____

_____

LESSON SIX

1. Carefully read through Chapter 6, "The Manifold Grace of God",
   page 71.

2. Explain how the believer is "sealed" by the Holy Spirit and its significance. _____

   _____

   _____

3. How is the Holy Spirit the "guarantee or earnest" of our inheritance?

   _____

   _____

   _____

4. Give a brief explanation of:

   a. 1 John 2:27 _____

   _____

   b. Ephesians 4:12 _____

   _____

5. Describe how the Holy Spirit helps us in our prayer life.

   _____

   _____

   _____

6. Why are we to pray and for what purpose?

   _____

   _____

   _____

7. Explain how true prayer moves in a cycle.

_____

_____

_____

8. In what ways does the Holy Spirit help us as we witness?

_____

_____

_____

9. In what three ways can the believer be a witness to the world today?

a. _____

_____

b. _____

_____

c. _____

_____

10. What is the primary work of the Spirit in the life of the believer and what is the key to this becoming a reality?

_____

_____

_____

LESSON SEVEN

1. Carefully read through Chapter 7, "Unity in Diversity", page 89.

2. In 1 Corinthians 12, Paul lists nine spiritual gifts. These gifts can be divided into three sections or "triplets". They are:

   a. _____

   b. _____

   c. _____

3. What important principle are we to always remember concerning the gifts of the Spirit? _____

   _____

   _____

4. Briefly explain these terms:

   a. "diversities of gifts" _____

   _____

   b. "differences of ministries" _____

   _____

   c. "diversities of operations" _____

   _____

5. Why is it important that we do not seek to duplicate another person's gift? _____

   _____

   _____

6. According to 1 Corinthians 12:7, what is the purpose for the manifestation of the Spirit? _____

   _____

7. Why does Paul encourage us in 1 Corinthians 12 to earnestly covet the "best gifts"? _____

_____

_____

8. What are the "best gifts"? _____

_____

_____

9. Why is it wrong for us to judge others in the way they may worship the Lord? _____

_____

_____

10. What promise is given to us in Luke 11:13 and how can we apply this to our lives? _____

_____

_____

LESSON EIGHT

1. Carefully read through Chapter 8, "The Word of Wisdom", page 99.

2. Explain briefly the difference between knowledge and wisdom.

_____

_____

_____

3. According the Psalm 111:10, what is true wisdom?

_____

_____

_____

4. Why is it a dangerous thing to have knowledge without wisdom?

_____

_____

_____

5. When and why do we need the word of wisdom?

_____

_____

_____

6. Why is this gift more than "wisdom in general"?

_____

_____

_____

_____

7. How did the Spirit manifest the gift of the word of wisdom in these situations:

a. 1 Kings 3:16-28 _____

_____

b. Luke 20:22-26 _____

_____

c. Acts 6:2-4 _____

_____

d. Acts 15:1-31 _____

_____

8. How can we recognize the word of wisdom operating in our lives?

_____

_____

_____

9. The gifts of the Spirit operate _____

_____

10. Why is it important for us to ask for the gift of the word of wisdom?

_____

_____

_____

LESSON NINE

1. Carefully read through Chapter 9, "How Did He Know That?", page 109.

2. Give a brief explanation of the gift of the word of knowledge.

_____

_____

_____

3. How was the word of knowledge exercised in the Old Testament, by Elisha, the prophet?_____

_____

_____

4. Describe the ways this gift operated in the lives of:

a. Jesus _____

_____

b. Peter _____

_____

c. Paul _____

_____

5. How does this gift operate in the church today?

_____

_____

_____

6. Why is this gift important for the church? _____

_____

_____

7. In what ways can the gift of the word of knowledge be exercised through the teaching of God's word? _____

_____

_____

8. How is the Spirit sovereign concerning His gifts?

_____

_____

_____

9. In what way does the Spirit operate in our lives?

_____

_____

_____

10. What is the purpose of this gift and why does God reveal His knowledge to us? _____

_____

_____

LESSON TEN

1. Carefully read through Chapter 10, "How to Plant a Mulberry Tree in the Ocean", page 119.

2. How does the writer of the book of Hebrews define faith?

_____

_____

_____

3. Briefly describe the differences between the three kinds of faith that are spoken of in scripture:

   a. Saving faith _____

   _____

   b. Faith that trusts in the promise of God _____

   _____

   c. Healing faith_____

   _____

4. How is "healing faith" related to what 1 Corinthians 12 calls the gift of faith? _____

   _____

   _____

5. Why is "selfish enrichment" the wrong motive for the gift of faith?

   _____

   _____

   _____

6. How can God give this gift for unique circumstances in our lives?

   _____

7. Faith is a gift of the Spirit endowing you with _____

_____

8. Why is faith only given by the Spirit for specific situations?

_____

_____

_____

9. How does the gift of faith relate to suffering and difficulties?

_____

_____

_____

10. For what purpose did God choose faith to be the conduit of our salvation? _____

_____

_____

11. Why is it important for the church to walk in faith?

_____

_____

_____

LESSON ELEVEN

1. Carefully read through Chapter 11, "Hope for the Sick", page 129.

2. Where does all healing come from? _____

   _____

3. Describe in your own words the meaning of Paul's exhortation given in 1 Corinthians 12:31. _____

   _____

   _____

4. What three actions are we to take concerning healing for the sick?

   a. _____

   _____

   b. _____

   _____

   c. _____

   _____

5. According to Genesis 20:17, what was Abimelech's problem and how was he healed? _____

   _____

   _____

6. What conditions did God place upon the children of Israel for their health? (Exodus 15:26) _____

   _____

   _____

7. Explain the meaning of Isaiah 53:5. _____

   _____

8. What were the signs of Jesus' relationship to the Father?

_____

_____

_____

9. Describe the commission by Jesus to His disciples in Matthew 10:8.

_____

_____

_____

10. What promises are we given in James 5:14-15?

_____

_____

_____

11. Why do we not see more divine healing today?

_____

_____

_____

12. What is the only explanation for lack of healing?

_____

_____

_____

13. According to 1 Peter 4:19, how should we respond to suffering?

_____

_____

_____

LESSON TWELVE

1. Carefully read through Chapter 12, "The Hardest Gift to Possess", page 139.

2. Give a brief explanation of a miracle. _____

_____

_____

3. Explain why our view of Genesis 1:1 is vital to our view of all miracles.

_____

_____

_____

4. Why do people try to explain away the miracles of the Bible? _____

_____

_____

_____

5. Briefly describe some of the miracles recorded in the Old Testament and in the New Testament:

Old Testament	New Testament
a. Exodus 14	d. Matthew 8
b. 2 Kings 4	e. Luke 5
c. Joshua 10	f. Acts 8

6. How can we be sure that the days of miracles are not over?

_____

_____

_____

7. Why is salvation also considered a miracle?

_____

_____

_____

8. What are some of the potential dangers of having the gift of miracles?

_____

_____

_____

9. What are some of the hindrances to our possessing the gift of miracles?

_____

_____

_____

10. Why should we earnestly covet the gift of the working of miracles for ourselves and for the church?

_____

_____

_____

LESSON THIRTEEN

1. Carefully read through Chapter 13, "Speaking Forth the Word of God", page 151.

2. Briefly explain the gift of prophecy in your own words.

_____

_____

_____

3. List three ways the gift was practiced in the early church:

   a. _____

   b. _____

   c. _____

4. Give some examples of the exercise of the gift of prophecy in the Old and New Testaments. _____

_____

_____

_____

5. What exhortation was given by Paul to Timothy concerning this gift?

_____

_____

_____

6. Why are women not prohibited from the office of prophet in the church today? _____

_____

_____

_____

7. Briefly explain the difference between the office of a prophet and the gift of prophecy. _____

_____

_____

8. Why are we encouraged to desire the gift of prophecy?

a. _____

b. _____

c. _____

9. In what ways does the gift of prophecy operate in our lives?

_____

_____

_____

10. Describe the rules that Paul gave to the church concerning the exercise of this gift. _____

_____

_____

11. What are the three scriptural bases for judging prophecy?

a. _____

b. _____

c. _____

12. Why should we have a clear understanding of 1 Corinthians 14:32?

_____

_____

_____

LESSON FOURTEEN

1. Carefully read through Chapter 14, "Unmasking the Evil One", page 163.

2. Why is it theoretically possible for two worlds to co-exist at the same time? _____

_____

3. Describe the spirit beings that are listed for us in Ephesians 6:12.

_____

_____

_____

4. What does 2 Corinthians 11:14 tell us that Satan is able to do?

_____

_____

_____

5. Why do we need the gift of discerning of spirits?

_____

_____

_____

6. How can we sense the power of darkness?

_____

_____

_____

7. What problems may exist with having the gift of discerning of spirits?

_____

8. "We need this gift of discerning of spirits so that we might know whether a man is speaking to us for _____ out of his own _____, or for _____."

9. Briefly give an example of the use of this gift in the life of either Peter or Paul. _____

_____

_____

10. What is the real danger of a false prophet and what methods does he/she use to deceive? _____

_____

_____

11. Why is it vitally important for us to follow the leading of the Holy Spirit? _____

_____

_____

12. The Holy Spirit is able and eager to help us discern:

a. good from _____

b. right from _____

c. truth from _____

LESSON FIFTEEN

1. Carefully read through Chapter 15, "An Affront to the Intellect; a Blessing to the Soul", page 173.

2. What ability is given to us through the gift of tongues?

_____

_____

_____

3. The Greek word we translate "tongue" is _____

4. Give a brief description of the meaning of language.

_____

_____

_____

5. What does the gift of tongues express?

_____

_____

_____

6. In 1 Corinthians 14:21 Paul quoted what text and why did he use it?

_____

_____

_____

7. Why was it impossible for Jesus to speak in an unknown tongue?

_____

_____

_____

8. Describe the languages that were being spoken on the Day of Pentecost. _____

_____

_____

9. Briefly describe the events in:

a. Acts 2:7,8, 11 _____

b. Acts 10:44-46 _____

c. Acts 19:1-6 _____

10. List three ways the gift of tongues are to be used in the life of the believer:

a. _____

_____

b. _____

_____

c. _____

_____

11. In what three ways did Paul restrict the use of tongues in the church service? _____

_____

_____

12. Because tongues are not the real issue, what is the real issue and the real manifestation of the Holy Spirit in the life of the believer?

_____

_____

_____

LESSON SIXTEEN

1. Carefully read through Chapter 16, "What Did He Say?", page 185.

2. What is the one gift the believer is told specifically to pray to receive?

_____

_____

3. Why is the gift of interpretation of tongues necessary?

_____

_____

_____

4. Describe the difference between "translation" and "interpretation".

a. Translation _____

b. Interpretation _____

5. What Greek word is used for "interpret"?

_____

_____

_____

6. According to Paul's direction in 1 Corinthians 14:28, what should be our responsibility if there is no one in the church service to give an interpretation of the gift of tongues?

_____

_____

_____

7. When is it necessary to have an interpretation?

_____

8. Describe ways in which this gift operates in the life of the believer.

_____

_____

_____

9. Give a brief description of the difference between the gift of interpretation of tongues and the gift of prophecy.

_____

_____

_____

10. In what ways may God use the exercise of this gift in the life of an unbeliever? _____

_____

_____

LESSON SEVENTEEN

1. Carefully read through Chapter 17, "Helps—the Quiet Ministry", page 195.

2. Why is the gift of helps so important to the body of Christ?

_____

_____

_____

3. How can we apply the principles given in Matthew 6:1 to the gift of helps?

_____

_____

_____

4. What can bring about an attitude of resentfulness in our ministries?

_____

_____

5. According to Colossians 3:17, how are we to serve?

_____

_____

_____

6. Give examples of those, from the Old Testament and the New Testament, who exercised the gift of helps.

Old Testament	New Testament
a.	c.
b.	d.

7. Explain Matthew 25:21 in relation to our service for the Lord.

_____

_____

_____

8. What are the three words that are translated "minister" and what are their meanings?

   a. _____

   b. _____

   c. _____

9. Why can true ministry only be fulfilled by the anointing of the Holy Spirit?

_____

_____

_____

10. Briefly describe what true service is and how Jesus set the example.

_____

_____

_____

11. How can we find true satisfaction and fulfillment in ministry?

_____

_____

_____

LESSON EIGHTEEN

1. Carefully read through Chapter 18, "Enough Milk, Already", page 205.

2. According to Ephesians 4:11, who has been given to the church to instruct in the Word of God? _____

_____

_____

3. How is 1 Corinthians 11:23 relevant concerning the gift of teaching?

_____

_____

_____

4. Teaching is a _____ of God, and we must depend upon _____ for its exercise.

5. What was the three-fold ministry of Paul?

_____

_____

_____

6. Explain the difference between the gift of preaching contrasted to the gift of teaching.

Preaching	Teaching

7. Why is the gift of teaching necessary in the church today?

_____

_____

_____

8. What is the purpose of the gift of teaching?

_____

_____

_____

9. Describe the purpose of the "pastor-teacher".

_____

_____

_____

10. Give examples of the gift of teaching from the Old Testament and from the New Testament.

_____

_____

_____

11. Why is the anointing of the Holy Spirit for teaching so necessary?

_____

_____

_____

12. What are some of the results of good, biblical teaching in the life of a believer?

a. _____

b. _____

c. _____

LESSON NINETEEN

1. Carefully read through Chapter 19, "Just Do It!", page 215.

2. Why does the body of Christ need those who exercise the gift of exhortation?_____

_____

_____

3. Give a brief definition of the gift of exhortation.

_____

_____

_____

4. How does 1 Thessalonians 4:1 demonstrate to us the gift of exhortation?_____

_____

_____

5. Give some examples of exhortation from the lives of these Old Testament prophets:

a. Isaiah_____

_____

b. Habakkuk _____

_____

c. Jeremiah _____

_____

6. How can we know that the gift of exhortation held an important place in the lives of those in the New Testament?

_____

7. In what ways can the gift of exhortation work in the church today?

_____

_____

_____

8. Why is this gift often a companion gift to the gift of prophecy?

_____

_____

_____

9. What are some of the many things the scripture exhorts us to do and why this is critical to our lives?

_____

_____

_____

10. Explain the results we could expect today, in the church, if more people were exercising the gift of exhortation.

_____

_____

_____

LESSON TWENTY

1. Carefully read through Chapter 20, "Keep It Simple", page 225.

2. Explain the spiritual law of giving. _____

_____

3. What promises has God given concerning the principles of giving?

    a. Luke 6:38 _____

    b. 2 Corinthians 9:6 _____

    c. Romans 11:35 _____

    d. Malachi 3:8-10 _____

4. Briefly explain the seven guidelines telling us how to give:

    a. _____

    b. _____

    c. _____

    d. _____

    e. _____

    f. _____

    g. _____

5. Describe the attitude of the Pharisees toward giving.

_____

_____

_____

6. What happens when God moves upon the hearts of His people to give?

_____

_____

7. Explain the word "cheerful" in 2 Corinthians 9:7.

_____

_____

_____

8. Briefly describe the story of Ananias and Sapphira found in Acts 5.

_____

_____

_____

9. Why did God take their lives?

_____

_____

_____

10. Why is Jesus our primary example of giving?

_____

_____

_____

11. What three things are we to give?

   a. _____

   b. _____

   c. _____

How is true giving a gift that keeps on growing? _____

_____

_____

LESSON TWENTY ONE

1. Carefully read through Chapter 21, "An Awesome Responsibility", page 235.

2. Why does government exist and what is its purpose?

_____

_____

_____

3. What is the highest form of government?

_____

_____

_____

4. Explain the name "Israel" and how it relates to governing.

_____

_____

_____

5. Why was the tabernacle important to the nation of Israel.

_____

_____

_____

6. Explain Romans 12:8 and 1 Corinthians 12:28.

_____

_____

_____

7. Describe some of the responsibilities of those who take care of the spiritual well-being of the church.

_____

_____

_____

8. What is the primary qualification for leadership in the body of Christ?

_____

_____

_____

9. What quality was Paul looking for in 1 Timothy 3:1-4, 6?

_____

_____

_____

10. Describe the rules given in God's word to those who would exercise leadership or a role of governing.

a. _____

b. _____

c. _____

11. Why is the role or gift of government an awesome responsibility?

_____

_____

_____

12. Who are the ones who can faithfully rule and/or govern others?

_____

_____

LESSON TWENTY TWO

1. Carefully read through Chapter 22, "A Ready Help in Time of Need", page 245.

2. Describe the gift of mercy _____

_____

_____

3. How does justice differ from mercy? _____

_____

_____

4. Explain how God exercised His mercy in the life of Lot and his family. (Genesis 19) _____

_____

_____

5. What do these scriptures tells us about the mercy of God?

a. Daniel 9:9 _____

b. Numbers 14:18 _____

c. Psalm 100:56 _____

d. Micah 7:187 _____

6. How does God describe Himself in Exodus 34:5-7?

_____

_____

_____

7. Why is mercy listed as one of the gifts of the Holy Spirit?

_____

_____

8. How do people act who have the gift of mercy?

_____

_____

_____

9. According to Romans 12:8, how should this gift be exercised?

_____

_____

_____

10. What is the parallel trait to the gift of mercy and why is it important?

_____

_____

_____

11. What happens when we are motivated by mercy?

_____

_____

_____

12. Why is showing mercy not an option, but a command?

_____

_____

_____

13. Describe the results we can expect when God plants His nature in us.

_____

_____

_____

LESSON TWENTY THREE

1. Carefully read through Chapter 23, "The Real Baptism of Fire", page 257.

2. What do the following scriptures tell us about the Holy Spirit?

   a. Luke 3:16 _____

   b. John 1:33 _____

   c. Acts 1:4_____

3. The baptism with the Holy Spirit is separate and distinct from

   _____

4. What is the obvious meaning found in John 20:22 when Jesus breathed on His disciples and said to them "Receive the Holy Spirit"? _____

   _____

   _____

5. How can we know that Peter received the indwelling of the Holy Spirit when Jesus breathed on him? _____

   _____

   _____

6. According to Acts 1:4-5, when did Jesus promise His disciples they would be baptized with the Holy Spirit? _____

   _____

   _____

7. When was this promise fulfilled? (Read Acts 2:1-4)

   _____

   _____

   _____

8. What does this tell us about their regeneration experience and their baptism with the Holy Spirit?_____

_____

_____

9. How can we know that these were separate and distinct experiences?

_____

_____

_____

10. Explain the three prepositions which are used to describe relationships with the Holy Spirit:

a. "with" _____

b. "in" _____

c. "upon" _____

11. What is the purpose for the baptism of the Holy Spirit? (Read Acts 1:8) _____

_____

_____

12. Briefly describe the events that took place in these passages in the book of Acts:

a. Acts 2 _____

b. Acts 8 _____

c. Acts 9 _____

d. Acts 10 _____

e. Acts 19 _____

13. How can we receive the baptism with the Holy Spirit today?

_____

LESSON TWENTY FOUR

1. Carefully read through Chapter 24, "Ask and You Shall Receive", page 269.

2. Describe the events that took place in the upper room on the day of Pentecost. (Acts 2:1-13) _____

_____

_____

3. Give a brief description of the promise given in Acts 2:38-39.

_____

_____

_____

4. To whom is the promise given?

_____

_____

_____

5. Why does the Holy Spirit come into our lives?

_____

_____

_____

6. How do we receive the gift of the Holy Spirit?

_____

_____

_____

7. Why is faith a necessity for receiving this promise?

_____

8. How can we become hindered in asking for the gift of the Holy Spirit?

_____

_____

_____

9. What steps can we take when we are challenged to doubt the work of the Holy Spirit in our lives?

   a. _____

   b. _____

   c. _____

10. What results can we expect when we begin to walk in the Spirit and give Him full rein in our lives?

_____

_____

_____

11. The Holy Spirit is God's gift to us to enable us to:

   a. _____

   b. _____

   c. _____

   d. _____

12. How can we be confident that we are in God's will when we ask for the gift of the Holy Spirit?

_____

_____

13. How can we show God our gratitude for filling us with His Spirit?

_____

LESSON TWENTY FIVE

1. Carefully read through Chapter 25, "A Torrent of Love", page 279.

2. Give a brief explanation of the proclamation Jesus made in John 7:37-39.

_____

_____

_____

3. What kind of thirst was He speaking about?

_____

_____

_____

4. What is the only way to find fulfillment? _____

_____

_____

5. Why is it crucial for our service to God that the Spirit be released as a mighty, gushing torrent? _____

_____

_____

6. How does God's Spirit desire to use us? _____

_____

_____

_____

7. What will be manifested in our lives as the Holy Spirit flows forth?

_____

_____

8. Briefly give a definition of the word "Agape".

_____

_____

_____

9. According to 1 Corinthians 13, what are some of the attributes of
   Agape? _____

_____

_____

10. What is the fruit of the Spirit and the eight terms used to define it
    that are listed in Galatians 5:22-23?

   The Fruit of the Spirit is: _____

   The terms used for the fruit:

   a. _____

   b. _____

   c. _____

   d. _____

   e. _____

   f. _____

   g. _____

   h. _____

11. What is the genuine evidence of the Holy Spirit within our lives?

_____

_____

_____

LESSON TWENTY SIX

1. Carefully read through Chapter 26, "The Ultimate Experience", page 289.

2. Why is the Christian life the "ultimate experience"?

_____

_____

_____

3. Why is there difficulty in explaining spiritual things to the "natural" man? (Read 1 Corinthians 2:14) _____

_____

_____

4. According to John 15:1-2, what is God looking for in our lives?

_____

_____

_____

5. How is fruit produced in the life of a believer?

_____

_____

_____

6. What kind of fruit is God looking for in our lives?

_____

_____

_____

7. Describe what happens when a branch is cut off from its source of life.

_____

8. What is the source of all our spiritual nourishment and energy?

_____

_____

_____

9. How is it that we can come into contact with God?

_____

_____

_____

10. What has God provided for us and how do we appropriate it?

_____

_____

_____

"And do not be drunk with wine, in which is
dissipation; but be filled with the spirit."
Ephesians 4:32.